BE AN EFFECTIVE COMMUNICATOR

PROFESSIONAL NETWORKING

DWAYNE HICKS

ROSEN PUBLISHING

NEW YORK

Published in 2022 by The Rosen Publishing Group, Inc.
29 East 21st Street, New York, NY 10010

First Edition

Portions of this work were originally authored by Suzanne Weinick and published as *Professional Connections: Learning How to Network*. All new material in this edition was authored by Dwayne Hicks.

Library of Congress Cataloging-in-Publication Data

Names: Hicks, Dwayne, author.
Title: Professional networking / Dwayne Hicks.
Description: New York : Rosen Publishing, [2022] | Series: Be an effective
   communicator | Includes bibliographical references and index.
Identifiers: LCCN 2021029141 (print) | LCCN 2021029142 (ebook) | ISBN
   9781499470239 (library binding) | ISBN 9781499470222 (paperback) | ISBN
   9781499470246 (ebook)
Subjects: LCSH: Business networks--Juvenile literature. | Online social
   networks--Juvenile literature.
Classification: LCC HD69.S8 H53 2022 (print) | LCC HD69.S8 (ebook) | DDC
   650.1/3--dc23
LC record available at https://lccn.loc.gov/2021029141
LC ebook record available at https://lccn.loc.gov/2021029142

Manufactured in the United States of America

Some of the images in this book illustrate individuals who are models. The depictions do not imply actual situations or events.

CPSIA Compliance Information: Batch #CWRYA22. For further information contact Rosen Publishing, New York, New York at 1-800-237-9932.

Find us on

CONTENTS

INTRODUCTION

Networking is creating personal relationships that are helpful to both parties. This is best done face-to-face. You might meet an acquaintance for coffee to talk about a new project. You might visit local shops to meet businesspeople in the community. You may even bump into a friend of a friend on the street. However, as the internet continues to evolve with new ways to connect users all over the world, networking will continue to change to use the new technology. These are all ways people start to build their professional networks. The key is to keep your contact information organized so that your network can propel you to succeed in your professional life. Networking is an important skill for job searching and career building.

You may not realize it, but you likely already have a good start on a professional network. Think of the people closest to you—parents, grandparents, older brothers and sisters, aunts and uncles, and friends of the family. Even your friends can be network contacts. These are often the first people we turn to when we are in need of help or support. But the list doesn't end there. Your network

You usually don't have to look far to find your network. It includes the people you love and respect. But your network doesn't need to end there.

may also contain coaches, teachers, religious leaders, and others you interreact with during a typical week. Even then, these are just the beginning steps in building your network.

Networking is applying your interpersonal skills in a professional setting to meet new people and make new connections. Every person that you know may some-day be a potential client, employer, or coworker. The key is to learn how to make your relationships work to your advantage and to capitalize on your network of contacts. You must be able to have conversations with individuals on a personal level in order to enhance your communication skills. This will be vital to building a career and establishing lifelong mentor relationships.

Social networking websites function as online communities that connect people with common interests, political or religious beliefs, shared backgrounds, and careers. The most successful of these online social networking sites is Facebook. Facebook has transformed the way people distribute information about themselves and receive information about their friends. The identity you create on Facebook is your global résumé.

In the age of Facebook and other social sites like LinkedIn and Twitter, social networking is a very public forum for building connections. Many experts believe that the intimacy of personal conversations is becoming a lost art. However, to get noticed in this vast network of people, you must be able to navigate the internet and have personal interaction skills. People who create their own profile or page on these online networking sites must learn to manage and display this information. As with any new skill, learning to network effectively takes practice and planning.

CULTIVATING CONTACTS

The casual conversations we have with friends are clearly different from the conversations we have with coworkers, employers, clients, and others we meet in the professional world. This is not to say that you can't be friends with your coworkers. In fact, a friendly work environment is preferable to one that's stuffy or even hostile. But all workers need to keep one thing in mind: I'm at work! And I need to act like it.

Even if your goal in speaking to someone is to ultimately get a job, making a personal connection is key to forming productive professional connections with others. When you meet someone for the first time, finding common interests or experiences will help change a stranger into a friend or professional colleague. The technique for making this transformation is the art of social interaction. There's no formula for creating a personal connection, but there are skills you can master in order to make the process work for you.

Networking is building connections on a personal level. For some people it's difficult to approach a stranger in a room full of people. The first step is to be yourself and allow others to see the real you. When you approach someone, you should do what you can to learn something about that person, and share something about yourself. You need to ask questions that prompt the other person to share information about themselves: "How long have you lived in California?" "Where did you go to school?" These are the types of questions that create a personal conversation and can give you information about the person's life, values, and interests. This helps you to form a personal connection with a new acquaintance.

Once someone shares information with you, you can

Networking can happen just about anywhere, whether at a professional or casual gathering.

share similar information with them about yourself. You may find that the person you've just met is interested in the same activities, and that can lead to a meaningful connection. You might let someone know that you're involved in groups or organizations pertaining to your mutual interests. Even mentioning that you've read a good book or article about a shared interest could lead to a stronger personal connection.

The goal of face-to-face interaction with new people is to form a personal connection to initiate a new friendship. This can be awkward for some people, but it's a skill worth practicing. It's critical to connect with people on a personal level in order to form new friendships, but this can also help you reach your goals on a professional level. New acquaintances might become the people who will provide you with feedback, advice, resources, and many other benefits. They might even become role models and mentors. Keep in mind that new acquaintances may come to you for similar reasons, and it's a good idea to keep a mutual channel of communication open, resulting in even stronger network connections.

NONVERBAL COMMUNICATION

Body language is a form of communication that we all use and interpret every day. Most of us do it subconsciously, but we can use body language to become better listeners. Nonverbal modes of communicating include facial expressions, body posture, tone of voice, hand gestures, and eye movements. These physical displays often tell us a lot about what another person could be thinking. Body language creates a social perception and can have an impact on the meaning of verbal communication.

Janine Driver, author of *You Say More Than You Think* and the founder and president of the Body Language Institute, located in Washington, D.C., says that we all have a natural ability to be successful at using and interpreting body language. "We just need to learn to tap into it." According to Driver, "Over 50 percent of what we communicate with others is nonverbal." Therefore, learning to use your body language can improve your ability to be confident in social situations.

Consider the handshake. It's a powerful first impression gesture that says, "Let's connect." A business handshake should be no more than three seconds. Your grasp should be firm but not overpowering. Smile, maintain eye contact, and pay attention to the other person's body language. A friendly handshake helps create a positive first impression and can help when trying to establish a new network connection.

Interpreting body language cues helps you make an accurate assessment of a person's intentions. Awareness of your own body language when communicating with others will help you appear confident and secure. Avoid negative forms of body language, such as slouching, yawning, avoiding eye contact, and looking at your phone. These will make you appear uninterested and unsure. Maintaining positive body language, as well as being a good listener, will

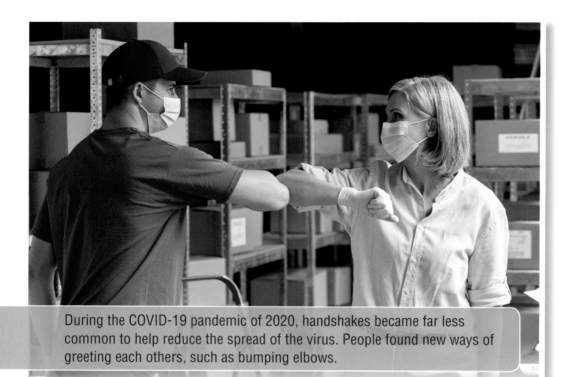

During the COVID-19 pandemic of 2020, handshakes became far less common to help reduce the spread of the virus. People found new ways of greeting each others, such as bumping elbows.

help you project your best self and help you build a strong professional network.

BE A GOOD LISTENER

When you're listening to someone give you information, you need to focus on what they're saying and process the information so that you can recall it later. Eye contact is important in connecting with what the speaker is saying. Don't be distracted by background conversations or unrelated activities around you. This will help you stay focused and assist your brain in recalling information received.

The information you gather from a new acquaintance

may be valuable to you in the future. That's professional networking! The more you remember about the other person, the better you will fare when you meet up again or come in contact with that person through social networking sites. If you remember where the person grew up, what pets they had, or something interesting about their family, it will show that you were listening when she spoke to you initially. It also shows that you can be a valuable network connection.

Being well-spoken is an important networking skill, but listening might be even more important.

Are We All Connected?

Hungarian author Frigyes Karinthy first came up with the idea that, as the world population increases, we are all at most 6 social connections away from everyone else on Earth. In the late 1960s, social psychologist Stanley Milgram researched the shortest path of acquaintances between two complete strangers; his limited studies, which he called the "small-world experiment," showed we are separated by 5.5 social links. Milgram's theory inspired the play *Six Degrees of Separation* by John Guare (which was also made into a movie).

By 1995, the idea that we are all somehow connected to each other became known as the six degrees of separation theory. People have developed games to measure the connections between actors (six degrees of Kevin Bacon) and musical artists (six degrees of Kanye West). Some researchers have shown that average social media connections are even lower than six degrees.

Columbia University professor Duncan Watts has studied network theory, the scientific field that examines how networks form and how they work in society. In 2004, Watts published the book *Six Degrees: The Science of a Connected Age*, which described the experiments he conducted. Professor Watts created an online experiment that assigned each "participant" a random "target" (one of 18 people around the world) to see how many emails it would take to get from someone the participant already knows to the target person. According to ABC News reporter Thomas Berman, approximately 60,000 people from more than 170 countries participated in the Small World Project as of December 2006, and the average number of links in the human chains was six. Therefore, the theory of six degrees of separation was proved with the use of the internet.

Naturally, the internet has been a perfect medium to prove

the hypothesis that we are all closely connected if we just use the links between us. Facebook, Twitter, and other social media platforms have been a catalyst in showing how close the relationships are to each other and how you can use this interconnectedness to network on a professional level.

ASSESS YOURSELF

Your personal goals and values influence the choices you make when deciding who to "friend" on Facebook and who you choose to connect with. However, most successful people will tell you that they became who they are because of the people they interacted with throughout their lives. Think of all the adults and leaders you interact with on a daily basis: parents and older siblings, high school and college counselors, teachers and mentors, coaches, employers, and leaders of volunteer organizations. These people help others reach their short-term and long-term goals. They are also a great resource for you when searching for a job that will utilize your specific skills and training.

Enhancing your personal networking skills is critical to becoming a successful adult. Making social and professional connections with others will prepare you for the challenges of job interviews, interacting with coworkers, obtaining a leadership position in the future, and much more. The goal is to build meaningful relationships without sacrificing your integrity or using other people only to attain your own objectives.

CHAPTER 2

CREATING A PROFESSIONAL NETWORK

It can be difficult to find a job coming straight out of school with little or no experience. It's especially tough if you don't have professional connections in your chosen field. Those who succeed in landing a job are often individuals who've invested the necessary time and effort into creating relationships that can help them prior to the commencement of their job search. You can start making professional connections while you're in high school, college, or graduate school. Every person you know is a contact who can help you find a job or further your career.

Not everyone knows what career field they want to enter after school. At some point, you'll decide what you want to do for a living as an adult. This can seem like an overwhelming challenge, but it can also be a time of personal growth. The best way to decide what path to take with respect to a career is to investigate areas that interest you. Knowing your strengths and weaknesses is critical to creating a successful plan of action. If you think you may be interested in a certain career, it's a good idea to seek experience in that field, even if it's as a volunteer, through an unpaid internship, or at an entry-level position during the weekends or summer vacation. This gives you the opportunity to be around other people who work in that field. It will also provide you with knowledge about technical skills and educational requirements needed to be successful in your chosen career.

Getting a part-time job as a teen will help prepare you for an adult career. It's a good idea to learn all you can from people more experienced than you.

Even as a teen, making professional connections will get you in the habit of looking at every new relationship as one that can enrich your life and your career path. You should approach others in a work environment with confidence and enthusiasm. It's critical to be punctual and give your full attention when going for an interview or attending a meeting or training session.

An important part of creating successful networking relationships is speaking in a strong voice with body language that reflects self-confidence. There are many subtle forms of body language that affect people's perceptions of each other. These include eye movements, hand gestures, facial expressions, and posture.

CONFIDENCE IS KEY.

For many people, breaking out of their comfort zone to approach a new contact and make a meaningful connection is difficult. Refusing to give into shyness and initiating a conversation will be uncomfortable at first. However, with practice, you will see how easy it can be to start a conversation with someone new.

You should be able to speak confidently about yourself, no matter who you're talking to—employers, teachers, friends, etc. If you find this hard to do, you can make a list of your skills and positive traits and be prepared to describe your educational background, your work experiences, and your personal interests. Present an image of yourself that reflects the skills you have, which in turn will help you project a feeling of confidence.

Creating a list of your skills and accomplishments can increase your confidence, but it can also help you discover your future career path.

Pick a Card

Business cards usually have only basic contact information on them: name, title, phone number, email, and office address. You can collect cards from other professionals and keep them in a safe place. It's a good habit to write on the back of someone's business card the information you obtain after talking to that person. For example, you may find out through a conversation with a company president that she loves swimming, is a former EMT, and has two teenagers. Recalling this information in a casual conversation with that individual will help move to a higher level in your relationship with that person. It will also make you more memorable.

Even though you may not get a business card from every new person you meet, it's important to get to know people on a personal level. You may find that the activities they participate in and the organizations they're involved in are things that you're interested in. These connections will give you a unique chance to reach out to that person in a personal way.

Not everyone needs or carries business cards. Especially today with so many forms of social media, people have fewer problems connecting with others and remembering important information about them. At the same time, however, presenting a business card to someone else displays a sense of traditional professionalism that many people appreciate. Also, a physical calling card might make you more memorable to some employers.

You can now order business cards that feature QR codes. People can scan your card with their smartphone and go to your website or Facebook page.

WHO'S IN YOUR AUDIENCE?

Whether you're on a job interview, at a business convention, or attending a career seminar, you'll be more relaxed if you're prepared before you go. Make sure you research the company and position for which you're applying, and learn about the industry you're networking within. This is called doing your professional homework by acquiring insight about current issues affecting a business or industry. The more knowledgeable you are regarding various news events and topics of interest, the easier it will be for you to make an informed statement if there's a pause in a conversation you're engaged in. The objective is to be prepared, and this will bolster your confidence.

Avoid being controversial when choosing a topic to discuss with new acquaintances. Demonstrate self-control when it comes to expressing opinions in a professional conversation. Ask questions that are appropriate to the setting and demonstrate that you have knowledge about the industry or business ideas being discussed. Being genuinely interested in what someone has to say will go a long way in keeping a conversation going. It will also help build interest in you as a potential employee.

FEEDBACK AND CRITICISM

Social networking would be less effective without soliciting feedback from others you work with. It can be an informal assessment of whether that person—whether they're a boss, a client, or coworker—believes that you've made contributions to a business meeting or discussion. Talk to your supervisor after you've completed a new task at your job or internship and ask them to review your performance.

Consider every new experience as a chance to grow and learn about how to improve your skills and abilities. Use the feedback to help you evaluate your own competence at making your mark on new contacts. You need to be open to criticism. Positive feedback can be turned into a reference for future jobs and opportunities. Constructive feedback will give you a chance to improve your skills to achieve your future goals.

NETWORKING OPPORTUNITIES

You can start building your professional network while in high school or college. When possible, take advantage of part-time jobs, volunteer opportunities, and internships, which will expose you to new networking contacts. They also give you a chance to explore different vocational choices you may be interested in.

People from all walks of life participate in community service. Volunteering provides the ability to practice and use leadership and organizational skills to make a difference in your community. By involving yourself in different types of activities, you open yourself up to working with people from different backgrounds. This will enlighten you about the common things that connect people, but it can also better prepare you for a full-time work environment. Local clubs, religious groups, and volunteer organizations are always looking for new participants to donate time and effort.

Joining, or forming, a volunteer group to clean up your neighborhood park is a great way to meet others with your interests, as well as businesspeople from the community.

The Pitfalls of Multitasking

Multitasking is the action of doing multiple tasks at the same time, with the intention of getting more work done in a shorter time. However, when you multitask, you sometimes interfere with the brain's ability to store information in short-term memory. The average person receives hundreds of messages every day via email, text messages, and television and radio advertisements. The sheer volume of information clouds our minds and makes it hard for us to concentrate on what's important. You may need to unplug and turn off personal electronic devices when you need to focus on one activity or project. Multitasking can also be costly and even deadly—never text while driving or operating equipment.

Maggie Jackson, author of *Distracted: The Erosion of Attention and the Coming Dark Age*, says multitasking causes "stress and frustration and lowered creativity" because the interruption causes the brain to experience attention fragmentation. Distracted texting, emailing, and blogging can make your words meaningless, or it can result in your words not conveying what you had hoped to convey. Jackson points out that multitasking makes us "less and less able to see, hear, and comprehend what's relevant and permanent." Once distracted, people often take time to return to the interrupted task. This is an unproductive habit that has a negative impact on critical thinking skills.

INTERNSHIPS

Internships are a great way to explore career interests and get work experience in a chosen field. Many of these opportunities are available for high school or college students. They're usually volunteer or low-paid, short-term positions. However, many internships lead to future employment opportunities. Internships are a perfect way to make contacts in industries of interest to you and to build your résumé. In order to get an internship, you may have to complete an application. But some internships are created when someone inquires about a position in a business that could use part-time help from someone willing to learn.

When asked how they ended up in their job or industry, many people will tell you that there were a series of fortunate events that led them to where they are today. These fortunate events are not coincidences because these same people were very good at networking with their peers, mentors, and colleagues. Unexpected professional opportunities can also arise out of community service activities and volunteer work.

BE AWARE OF YOUR ENVIRONMENT

As an employee in any industry, whether it's in an entry-level position or a job you've worked at for a long time, you should be aware of what's happening in the organization. Every office or work environment has an institutional culture. You'll need to communicate with coworkers and superiors to determine the way things are done in the office, factory, or store. Ask questions before you make a mistake—don't be overconfident. If you're not sure how the company you're working for does something, find out from someone who knows. For example, you should know what the procedures are for taking time off to see a doctor. Do you need to get approval from a superior? Will you need a note from your doctor as proof of the visit? Some organizations or work environments are highly structured and others are more flexible. It is critical to exhibit a strong work ethic. This means you get to meetings on time, you learn the names of coworkers, and you avoid taking the easy way out when a task is presented.

Make people aware of your presence. When attending conventions, trade shows, and meetings, your goal should be to make new contacts and pay attention to name tags. Oftentimes, you'll find an immediate connection to people. Other times, you will have to work at finding a common interest.

When possible, it's a good idea to meet casually with your coworkers, whether it's a quick lunch or a weekend outing. Getting to know your coworkers can help improve working relationships.

MYTHS and facts

MYTH

Shy people can never be good networkers.

FACT

Shy people can be just as good at networking as outgoing people. They just need to work on it. Introverts are usually people who need to be confident before they speak about something. If you do your research before you approach new people, you'll gain the self-confidence to enter new relationships and form lasting network connections. Practice speaking out loud to your friends and you'll gain the ability to speak publicly with strangers. Many schools offer courses in public speaking, which is a valuable skill no matter what career path you choose.

MYTH

Networking online is the same as networking face-to-face.

FACT

Social media has become a valuable tool for networking and finding work. However, face-to-face interaction allows individuals to connect on a deeper level than on social networking sites. You can read someone's body language, change topics more rapidly, and connect with someone in a more personal manner. People remember faces differently than they remember words and names. If you want to stand out from the crowd, it's a good idea to make an impression on someone by meeting them in person.

MYTH

You can say whatever you want online because it's a medium of true expression.

FACT

The internet is an open public forum. This, of course, is a good thing, but if you say negative things about someone—for example, a difficult high school teacher—those words may come back to haunt you when they're discovered by a potential employer or a college scholarship committee. For all its positive attributes, providing free access to information sharing around the world, the internet also a place where words and images never go away. Be aware that there's always an online trail that leads back to you.

ONLINE NETWORKING

CHAPTER 3

High school and college students today experience campus life in both the real and virtual world. For example, most high school students will meet their college roommates online before they meet them in person at an orientation. Students all over the world can share information about clubs, social causes, political activism, and events on campus through social networks online and on mobile devices. Each time a student joins an online group, posts a comment or picture, or participates in an online conversation, that student has to decide if their response or participation will be appropriate and ethical. These can be very difficult decisions to make, but your online reputation depends on it.

Employers and employment search companies make liberal use of social networking sites like Facebook, Twitter, and LinkedIn to search for potential candidates with specific educational backgrounds, past experience in certain fields, and a geographic location convenient for job placements. Other popular social media sites include Instagram, WhatsApp, and Pinterest. It's critical that your profile on a social networking site accurately reflects your job experience, educational degrees, and expertise in your field. It's also important to avoid adding too many personal details.

In 2020, during the COVID-19 pandemic, many business continued to have meetings through online conferencing platforms such as Zoom. While these platforms aren't social media, they did help people stay in touch and keep their networks strong.

NETWORKING WITH FACEBOOK

Facebook might be the first social networking site most people think of. Facebook started as a personal network to help college students stay in touch with friends. However, it has expanded its scope to include connecting people based on prior business contacts, which could lead to finding a job or connecting with a professional community.

Learning to use Facebook to your advantage is a great way to build solid social networks with people who can enhance your life. Posting messages on your online wall can prompt your online friends to interact with you. Reading other people's messages many lead you to new contacts and provide leads for educational or business opportunities. If someone is looking for help and you give them assistance, you'll find that most of the people you collaborate with will give you guidance when you ask for it.

Facebook is a less formal social networking website for personal interaction between people who already know each other. If you're constantly going online to solicit a job or advice regarding a personal matter rather than keeping it casual, you may find that others might defriend or ignore you. Facebook tends to be about continued positive interaction between online friends

Keep in mind that Facebook is a very public social networking site, and privacy settings are never airtight. Your employer may be able to view your photos, posts, and list of friends, even if you haven't become friends with them on Facebook. Keep that in mind.

NETWORKING WITH TWITTER

Twitter is a unique social networking platform that allows users to share real-time short messages. These "tweets," once no more than 140 characters, can now have up to 280 characters, allowing people to share snippets of their thoughts and experiences. Twitter is a microblogging format that allows a person to "follow" a person, organization, group, or business. Twitter can be used as an efficient way to send microposts to a group of subscribers or publicly on the website itself. The social networking component of tweets is that they allow you to express your opinion or your knowledge on a topic or product. The benefit is that if you share your knowledge with others, they will share their knowledge with you. When applied correctly, there's a good chance that this type of communication could enhance your networking circle.

Companies sometimes post job openings on Twitter, and talented people have been offered opportunities based on interesting tweets. However, many people just use Twitter to chat about their weekend plans, fashion picks, celebrity sightings, and friendship drama. If this is what you're tweeting about, you

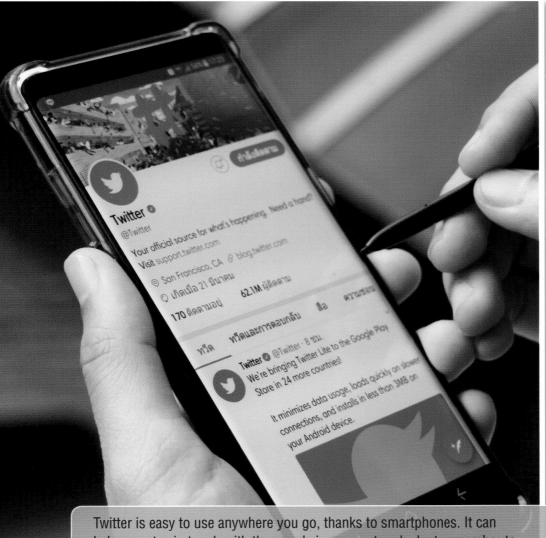

Twitter is easy to use anywhere you go, thanks to smartphones. It can help you stay in touch with the people in your network. Just remember to keep your tweets appropriate and interesting.

should not include professional contacts in your subscriber list. Use another form of social media, like LinkedIn, to keep business acquaintances informed about your status and appropriate information about you.

More About Facebook and Twitter

Facebook is a privately held company founded in 2004 by Mark Zuckerberg. It was created as a way for students at Harvard University to communicate with each other. In 2006, Facebook was made available to everyone. You start by creating a profile with information about yourself where friends, family, classmates, and acquaintances can find you. Once people add you as their friend, you have access to their lives as they exist on their Facebook "wall."

Facebook has been plagued with complaints about privacy issues. It created a new set of privacy controls in 2009. However, users complained that figuring out the privacy settings was too complicated. Zuckerberg has been criticized for being insensitive about third-party access to information shared on Facebook. Ironically, on January 31, 2011, Zuckerberg obtained a restraining order against a man who was harassing him. Since then, Facebook has gone through other updates, acquisitions, controversies, and legal issues. Despite its problems, Facebook has revolutionized the way people socialize.

In 2006, a podcasting company in San Francisco, California, started Twitter. Jack Dorsey, Twitter creator, cofounder, and chairman, was determined to blend email and instant messaging to create "status information" in a web-based format. Twitter is a short-messaging service inspired by text messages on cell phones. Twitter allows users to send tweets, or messages no longer than 280 characters, on its website to anyone who wants to "follow" them. Dorsey sent the first tweet on March 21, 2006.

Twitter has become a powerful and popular marketing tool for businesses, political activists, and even celebrities. Twitter is free, but you must register in order to post messages. Twitter connects strangers with common interests. According to the *New York Times*, Twitter creates real-time commentary on daily activities. In 2009, people in Iran and Moldova organized government protests through Twitter. The 2011 uprising in Egypt is also credited to the use of Twitter and Facebook. In May 2020, Twitter users were sending 500 million tweets per day. That's about 6,000 tweets per second!

MARK ZUCKERBERG

JACK DORSEY

NETWORKING WITH LINKEDIN

LinkedIn, a professional social network that was started in 2003, allows professionals to connect with one another. LinkedIn users set up a profile containing their educational background, work experience, and expertise. LinkedIn is interesting because when you connect with people on it, their profile pages show the people, companies, and organizations they're already connected to. That opens a world of additional contacts for you.

LinkedIn has become a primary source for recruiters to look for candidates to fill a job opening. Many Fortune 500 companies have members on LinkedIn. Even nonprofit organizations have joined LinkedIn to find corporations and individuals to provide needed funding for projects. The LinkedIn site has become useful to entrepreneurs and consultants around the world who are interested in increasing their exposure to new opportunities.

While Facebook and Twitter are sometimes used for professional networking, LinkedIn is devoted to it. It's the world's largest professional network. Today, many people have a LinkedIn profile, and it's important to have a presence there for those seeking job opportunities and career connections. You do have to be 16 to have a profile.

Your professional profile should use keywords that hiring managers and recruiters use to find candidates. Look at profiles of other people in your career field to see what keywords are used in your industry or profession. You can get recommendations from close contacts to add credibility to your profile. LinkedIn allows users to join up to 50 groups within the site. Many job postings are listed within groups.

LinkedIn is a good online platform for connecting with industry peers and sharing your ideas and professional aspirations. Business leaders on LinkedIn may be a source of years of training and expertise if you connect with the right people. Creating these professional connections before you need them is a smart move.

Regardless of which personal and professional social networking sites you choose to join, your online profiles should be consistent. There is database crossover between your contacts on personal social networking sites and professional networking sites. Facebook and LinkedIn are the largest and most popular online social networks, but there are many others that are useful. Based on your career aspirations, you can find communities through professional organizations and career-oriented sites.

KEEP IN TOUCH.

Networking for your future is a constant job that takes effort. Keeping in touch with the connections you've made is essential to expanding your personal network. You need to keep in touch with people you knew from high school and college—including teachers, coaches, and mentors. Traditional methods of communication, such as letter writing and telephone calls, are becoming obsolete. In our modern times, Facebook and school-based social networks will help maintain your connections. However, don't

Meeting with colleagues face-to-face has never been easier; you don't even need to leave your house! Video communications apps such as Zoom, Skype, and Google Hangouts help connect people in distant locations.

bombard your contacts with too many messages. General updates about your current employment status and what you're working on may be enough to keep people informed but not overburdened by your status.

Online communications require appropriate protocol. You should treat people with respect and remember that networking is a two-way street. The benefit of all online social networks is that they provide you with constant access to a global community. Facebook, LinkedIn, and Twitter can be used on a computer, smartphone, or tablet. This means you can always be connected with your family, friends, colleagues, and contacts. However, always be aware of your audience and the content, style, and tone of your messages.

Professional networking sites allow you to create an online résumé with your education and work experience. However, this won't reveal your unique personality. Only in-person meetings will allow you to present yourself fully. Connecting online is certainly a great start to a relationship, but it won't reach its full potential until you meet face-to-face.

Online social networking sites will continue to grow and change as users interact with each other. Privacy and profile management are major issues that will affect which social networking sites survive and which thrive.

10 Great Questions
TO ASK A GUIDANCE COUNSELOR

1. I'm afraid of public speaking, though I know it's important for my career. How can I get over my fear?

2. What are the benefits of an internship, and where can I find one?

3. How do I begin looking for places to make professional connections?

4. How can getting involved in my community help me make professional connections?

5. How should I organize my personal and business contacts?

6. How can I safely use social networking sites to promote myself?

7. What are the best sites to use to create a profile showing my skills and experiences?

8. How do I post my information on the internet without risking identity theft?

9. How should I dress for a professional interview?

10. What body language should I use to show a speaker that I'm listening?

ETIQUETTE AND SAFETY ONLINE

Social networking is the process of using web-based tools to connect with people. It's a great way to stay connected with friends and family, but it can also be used to reach your career and business goals and help others reach their goals as well. The benefits of using the internet for personal and professional success are enormous, with all of the discussion groups, blogs, social networking sites, and message boards that are available. However, social networking online can also be a huge, time-consuming activity with pitfalls that every user should be aware of.

Spending too much time on social media can have a negative impact on your personal and professional lives. Many employers won't tolerate workers wasting company time reading Facebook posts.

Social networking websites provide an online community. These web-based communities connect people with shared interests, hobbies, political views, careers, and ideas. One huge advantage of online networking over in-person networking is that you have unlimited access to millions of contacts. The big disadvantage to social networking on the internet is that you need to build trust in your online relationships in a different way. Your online identity must be created carefully and protected at all times. It's important to control how people get your contact information online. Most social networking sites allow users to determine their privacy settings.

Employers, recruiters, and colleges use social networks and search engines like Google to do "unofficial" background checks on potential employees and high school students applying for admission. Remember: Everything you say or post online leaves a digital trail that can influence your reputation and character—for good or bad. Never air your frustrations or put personal or social activities online that could detract from your professional reputation. Remember that social networking is a way to market yourself to a broader community of potential employers, clients, and business contacts. So it's vital that you follow some rules as you dive into professional networking online.

BEFORE YOU WRITE

Writing is a fundamental communication skill, even now when traditional communication methods such as writing letters are considered archaic. But online writing is a very common form of communicating today. Unlike reading, listening, and talking, writing is difficult for many people. There are clear advantages to written communication over the other forms of communication because you have the opportunity to review and revise the written word before you share it or send it to others. You have time to make sure your message is consistent, logical, and clear.

When you're building your social network, you should write to new contacts in a direct and concise manner. Always check your spelling and grammar so that your message is the thing that stands out to the recipient, not your lack of writing skills. If you want to be taken seriously, you need to be adept at composing a well-written email or letter. Get in the habit of sending thank-you notes or emails to contacts who have assisted you in achieving your professional goals.

GET ORGANIZED

If you've made important networking contacts with whom you exchange emails, you may want to organize your emails in folders. If you leave emails in your inbox, you may forget to respond to them or you may accidentally delete them. Always respond promptly to emails, even if your response is that you don't have the answer to a question yet but you received the request. In addition, don't harass a new contact with numerous emails. Keep your communications simple and short.

Also, you may want to set up different email addresses

Email apps help you organize your correspondance with others. Most have features that allow you to sort contacts, prioritize tasks, and schedule important meetings in a planner.

for different purposes. One email should be for personal cor-respondences, and another should be for job searches and professional contacts. This will keep your inbox organized and your business and personal correspondence separate.

You may want to create another email address for sign-ing up for online newsletters, shopping sites, and general correspondences with businesses that you don't have an individual contact for. Then you can more effectively view your emails and filter out those you don't want to continue to receive, without compromising your entire email account.

SEARCHING THE WEB

The internet is an amazing resource for information and net-working. However, any content posted on the web should be viewed with skepticism based on the source of the informa-tion. The problem is that anyone can post, comment, blog, and write on the internet, and it's difficult to determine the expertise or knowledge of those "experts" online. Therefore, you must be cautious when relying on information found on the internet. You should filter out content that's posted by groups and organizations that are trying to persuade you to buy, vote on, or think differently about a topic or product.

Google is the leading search engine on the internet. Performing a Google search can lead to a plethora of sources of information. This includes newspapers, magazines, trade publications, university guides, and more. Keeping up with the latest news about an industry will help you break into that industry in the future. YouTube is another social media

C. Burr Artz
301-600-1630
www.fcpl.org

- Checkout Receipt -

Patron Barcode: **********6384

Number of items: 5

Barcode: 31982020029486
Title: Escape plan: The extractors /
Due: 11/21/2023

Barcode: 31982020116614
Title: Amadeus /
Due: 11/21/2023

Barcode: 21982319251496
Title: Succeed with social media like a creative genius : a guide for artists, entrepreneurs, inventors, an
Due: 12/05/2023

Barcode: 21982319150235
Title: Never too old to get rich : the entrepreneur's guide to starting a business mid-life /
Due: 12/05/2023

Barcode: 21982320621331
Title: Professional networking /
Due: 12/05/2023

11/14/2023 01:47:03 PM

Many people online claim to be something they are not. It can be almost impossible to know for sure sometimes. It's your job to be on guard for scams and identity theft.

site that engages people through video posts. While some videos are entertaining and others are instructional, it's still wise to be careful which videos you trust as fact and which are just trying to sell you something.

CAN WE CHAT?

You can locate valuable sources of information in online forums and message boards. Forums are places where people meet online in real time to talk about a topic. Forums and message boards are usually organized by special interests or general subject matters. You can visit message boards and read previous conversations (called threads) on a particular topic or question. You can use Google search engine to locate and access forums and message boards that cover topics of interest to you. You can visit a specific website for a subject, hobby, or interest that you're looking to obtain more information about. These resources allow people to form an interactive community that is the essence of social networking.

People who share your interest in a hobby or leisure activity will likely be people who share at least something of your idea of the perfect job or career. You should look to develop relationships with individuals who have common interests. These contacts are often a great resource for future job searches. You can build a connection of mutual trust and reliability that could lead to other ways of connecting on a professional and personal level.

Many people read messages on their personal electronic

devices and don't have time for lengthy explanations. Your online communications should be direct and clear. Make your emails, posts, and messages useful and productive. Depending on your goal, you may want to ask questions that elicit a response from the reader.

Never reveal your personal information on a message board or in a forum. Despite how professional an online community may appear to be, there are people who might pose as professionals to take advantage of you. With this in mind, never agree to meet with someone you just connected with online without your adult guardian's knowledge.

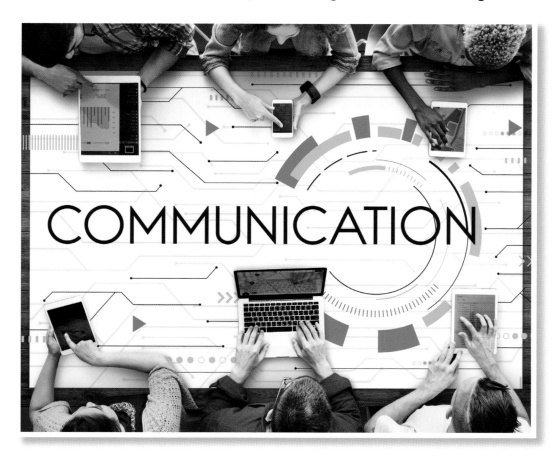

Discord

Discord is a highly popular free app that millions of people use to chat through texts, voice, and videos. Discord servers are private meeting areas where you need to be invited by another member. This allows you to create small groups of friends and acquaintances who share common interests. Gamers love Discord for creating a meeting place to play *Minecraft*, *Fortnite*, and many other games. Families use Discord to stay in touch with each other. Teachers can use Discord to tutor students.

Anyone can start a Discord server for free. This is a specific place where people can meet. Most are small groups by invitation only, but some larger servers have become popular with people all over the world. Servers are organized in channels, which are devoted to certain topics. Discord offers both text and voice channels. Users can also share their screen with others on the server. Gamers use this to show off their skills, but the feature can also be used to conduct meetings.

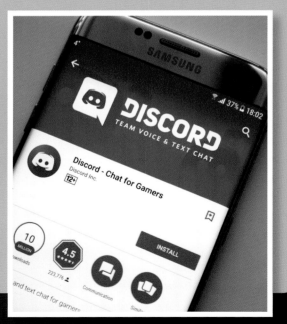

ONLINE DANGERS

The ease with which we send emails, texts, and social media posts makes it tempting to be constantly in touch with friends, family, and coworkers. Information overload can lead to making bad choices and costly mistakes. Constantly viewing incoming messages and replying to all of them makes it difficult for many people to live in the moment and focus on the task at hand. Just because someone sends you a message doesn't mean you need to respond instantly. Sometimes it's important to think about new information in order to provide an accurate and thoughtful response.

If you have difficulty processing excessive information, you should silence your phone or computer messaging feature while you're concentrating on something that needs your full attention. Posts on Facebook and Twitter tweets will be there after completing an assignment or project requiring your full concentration. It's important to take advantage of modern technology, but you can't let it rule your life.

If you're the messenger, in the interest of efficiency and time, you need to keep your online communications meaningful and concise. You can embrace the new technologies associated with social networking without becoming overwhelmed by it. Don't let yourself get drown in the nonstop stream of information online.

The internet is a limitless source of information, but when online, you need to be careful with your personal information. There is the problem of online predators and individuals who create fictitious identities. You should be very careful about the amount of personal information you put online. Remember that the internet is uncensored, and not everyone is who they say they are online.

Online identity theft is a huge concern. You must beware of scams and spam on the web that could cause you to give your personal information to strangers. Legitimate websites usually require you to log on to interact with others. You should not share your passwords with anyone. Use common sense and don't open email attachments that you're not expecting.

Cyberbullying is a problem on social networking sites. Studies have shown that more than 50 percent of adolescents and teens have been bullied online; about the same number have reportedly engaged in cyberbullying. If you experience cyberbullying, inform the social networking site manager and tell an adult you trust. Avoid environments that make you more susceptible to risks, stay on reputable websites, and communicate only with people you know or have been referred to by someone you respect.

Online social networking should not become a substitute for connecting with people in person. There are dangers in developing relationships with people you meet online. After you've engaged in dialogue with new contacts online, you should work on building a significant level of trust before you meet someone in person. Online communities have evolved to provide forums for those with common interests and ideas. It's smart to make your initial in-person connection with someone you met online in a public location, such as a convention, club meeting, or large public gathering. This will

In 2020, the FBI received 791,790 complaints regarding cybercrime. This is about 300,000 more complaints than they received in 2019. Clearly, cybercrime is on the rise and everyone should be on guard.

afford you the opportunity to work on your face-to-face inter-personal skills while staying safe.

INFORMATION FOR SALE!

Social networking sites know that the information you provide online is valuable to advertisers and marketing firms. Because of this, much of your profile information is public, including the music you like, your shopping preferences, and your employment information. All the things that you "like" on Facebook become public information. To make your profile more private, you have to opt out of certain Facebook applications; it can be very complex to figure all of this out. The only way to truly protect your privacy on Facebook is to limit how you use it. It's a good idea to use Facebook only to connect with actual friends, family, and colleagues. Use your web browser to conduct searches for products, information, and music.

You're responsible for what you post online. Posting lies or cyberbullying can have serious legal consequences. Law enforcement will prosecute for some inappropriate and bullying postings online. Students have been suspended from school or prosecuted for underage drinking or using drugs because of pictures posted on Facebook. It's becoming more common for schools to discipline students and staff for behavior conducted online. In general, there is limited privacy on social networking sites.

FINDING SUCCESS WITH NETWORKING

CHAPTER 5

Many professionals believe that networking is the number-one job search strategy. Although some people feel awkward and nervous about reaching out to a potential contact, most people enjoy talking about their jobs and are willing to give realistic, and free, advice. Therefore, it's essential to practice the art of networking. It will pay off in the long run.

It's critical to make time to expand and enhance your professional network. You will need to be organized and to prepare for meeting people in your career. Many experts suggest that you keep a network

It's always a good idea to act professionally in the workplace, but that doesn't mean you can't enjoy your job and coworkers. Networks grow stronger as you get to know the people around you.

log of new contacts and information about them. You should schedule brief meetings with people in your network on a regular basis and not only when you need a job.

Another element vital in building a strategic network is to be a good listener. Ask questions about what the person

does in their job and how the person has moved up successfully within the company. Listening to the answers to these questions may provide you with information on how to handle your own career opportunities.

THE ART OF LISTENING

Listening is vital to successful communication. When you show people that you're concentrating on what they're saying, you make them feel validated and valued. Psychologist Michael P. Nichols says in *The Lost Art of Listening*, "The importance of listening cannot be overestimated." Nichols encourages people to be "reflective listeners." This requires being open, receptive, and flexible in paying attention to conversations. The value of being a good listener is that you will earn respect from those around you.

You should refrain from speaking when gathering information. This is known as supportive listening. When you engage the speaker by concentrating on what they're saying, the speaker is more likely to keep speaking to you. If you're distracted, the speaker may not want to continue conversing with you. Being a good listener means that you're actively

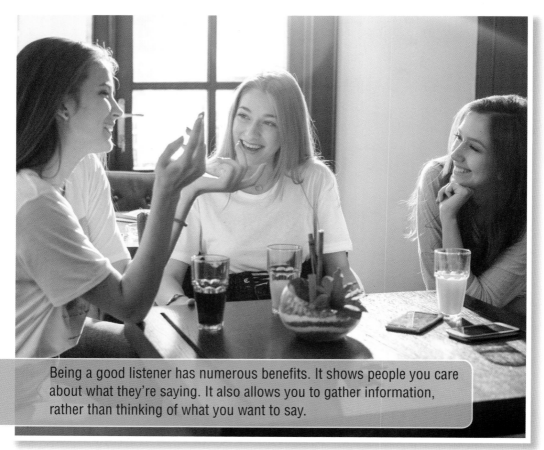

Being a good listener has numerous benefits. It shows people you care about what they're saying. It also allows you to gather information, rather than thinking of what you want to say.

trying to retain the information that's being presented to you. Instead of waiting for your turn to talk, try to think of follow-up questions you can ask the speaker when they finish speaking on a topic. This demonstrates to the speaker that you've been listening to what they are saying and that you would like additional information.

Remember that listening requires that the listener be alert and focused and make eye contact with the speaker. Resist the urge to debate the speaker, but use the opportunity to respond to the speaker in a manner that conveys that you've been paying attention.

Networking Dos and Don'ts

Here is a helpful list of behaviors you should and should not practice when building a strong professional network.

- Project confidence, but don't be arrogant or pushy.

- Be friendly to new acquaintances without appearing too anxious or obtrusive.

- Know your strengths and be able to discuss them.

- Be patient. Building a successful network of contacts takes time.

- Be creative. Explore new ways to connect with others through groups and online.

- Get to the point—don't waste other people's time.

- Don't get too personal in professional settings. Keep your personal life to yourself.

- Don't gossip and swear, and avoid being a negative person.

- The quality of your contacts is more important than the quantity.

- Always be ready to offer your help and share your knowledge with network contacts.

GET INVOLVED

Teens are often encouraged to join clubs, participate in athletics, and help out in their community. This is your entrance into getting to know your classmates, teachers, and leaders in your neighborhood. These are fertile settings for developing a social network and for setting a foundation for your future networking contacts. Note that it's critical to make connections with people who are older than you, not just your peers. This will give you chances to broaden your community network.

Community service teaches leadership skills and gives you the opportunity to work with all types of people. Organizations such as the Kiwanis, Lions, and Rotary International are community groups that combine social activities with community service. Joining these organizations is an easy way to connect to your community and increase your social network. There are local and national nonprofit groups and associations that will teach you to be an advocate for causes you're interested in promoting. Many professionals also volunteer for not-for-profit organizations; this could lead to connecting with people with similar interests and backgrounds.

There are many ways to meet new people, not just through professional associations. Many individuals feel comfortable connecting with new people through athletics, church, or political action committees. In these informal settings, you can find many networking opportunities. Remember that any community or social gathering is an opportunity to work

Playing a team sport is a great way to build a network of friends and mentors. You also learn a lot about teamwork, leadership, and pursuing goals.

on your networking skills. Networking requires action, and just sitting at your computer simply won't bring you the same results as getting out there and meeting people.

WHAT IT TAKES TO SUCCEED

Whether you're preparing for a college interview, a job interview, or a work meeting, experts agree that writing your ideas and questions on paper will help you convey your information clearly. Prior to the meeting, create a list of the points you want to make. This will help you stay focused and keep you from rambling and sounding unprepared. It's also a good idea to practice what you plan to say in front of a friend, teacher, or coworker that you trust to give you good feedback. You may even practice in front of a mirror. These techniques will help you find your voice and make networking easier for you.

There's a fine line between making new connections to enhance your career or personal goals and becoming someone who's always looking for something for yourself (like a job or an advantage in a situation). Your network of acquaintances won't make introductions for you if you abuse the relationships that you already have. Your motives for meeting new people should be to build your relationships, not just for selfish reasons. Remember that network relationships need to be a two-way street; you need to give before you receive.

There are many resources available to you to become a successful networker. (You will find some in the sections

Don't hesitate to reach out to network contacts you haven't talked to in a while. You may find they could use your help.

of this book titled "For More Information" and "For Further Reading.") Offering to exchange information with others will strengthen your relationships and shows goodwill. Chances are that you can make connections between people in your own social network that will lead to others making a useful connection for you.

Your inner circle of friends, family, and mentors are the people you can always turn to for advice, help, and support. When you share your opinions and ideas with new contacts, you bring them in closer to your inner circle. Always strive to

Every network connection you make connects you with that person's network. You never know how this could benefit you in the future.

make a good impression on the people you meet on a day-to-day basis. You want the buzz about you to always be positive. You're in control of your reputation, whether it's in person, at professional or social gatherings, or online when you chat and post with friends.

How you treat others around you is a reflection of who you are as a person. Be genuine and sincere, and people will respond to you in a favorable way. Are you respectful to your parents and siblings in public? Do you treat your coworkers fairly? Do you thank people who do things for you? These are good habits to follow when presenting your best self to the people around you.

LIFELONG CONNECTIONS

Building a network of contacts is a lifelong journey that begins when you're young. By constantly opening yourself up to new experiences and staying true to your goals, you'll succeed in creating a strong professional network. Take advantage of opportunities to grow, such as internships and community service. Being involved in a hobby or sport often leads to meeting someone who will give you a job or suggest a new path that you should take. You may have to overcome the anxiety of talking face-to-face with a stranger, but if you push yourself to do it, you'll find it gets easier with time and practice.

In order to be successful at networking, you must improve your organizational skills. Remember that your success in being an effective networker is directly connected to your ability to be perceived as someone who's honest and hard working. Finding

Success in the professional world is most often the result of a team of workers coming together to get the job done.

a trusted mentor is valuable in helping you gain perspective on what works for you while sharpening your networking skills.

Millions of people around the globe spend a great deal of time on social networking sites, searching for people and experiences. The connections being made will be lasting if the relationships between the people are real and relevant. If you want to be taken seriously, the information you put out must be beneficial to someone personally or professionally. Real network connections come from turning those online social networking connections into face-to-face interactions.

Networking is most successful when you're helping others first. You'll feel a sense of fulfillment when you participate in a meaningful way with your community. You may find that your experience creating new and valuable relationships could actually change your life. Virtual connections cannot replace physical connections between individuals and groups looking to make lasting connections. Life is all about the relationships we make and keep.

Always be yourself when interacting with others. Don't join clubs, attend meetings, or participate in community events if you're not truly interested in them. You won't be motivated and driven to be good at something if you're doing it only because you think you should or you believe that others want you to do it. If you want to learn to be a leader, you must first be a follower and a student.

This is where your skills at listening and organization will be instrumental. If you're passionate and energetic when you volunteer, perform your job, or prepare for school, the reward will be that others around you will catch your enthusiasm.

The better you are at building strong and lasting personal and professional relationships, the more successful you will be in life. Good communication skills will lead you to accomplishing your goals. Strong relationships are developed over time, and meaningful relationships are worth the time and effort it takes to develop them.

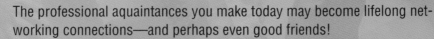

The professional aquaintances you make today may become lifelong net-working connections—and perhaps even good friends!

activism A doctrine or practice that emphasizes direct and vigorous action especially in support of or opposition to one side of a controversial issue.

blog An online journal kept by an individual, group, or website to record activities or conversations regarding a particular topic.

body language Nonverbal communication through the use of facial expressions, posture, and gestures.

colleague A fellow worker in a profession.

communication A process by which information is exchanged between individuals through a common system of symbols, signs, or behavior.

Discord A free voice, video, and text chat app where people can meet in invite-only spaces called servers.

Facebook A social networking website using customized individual profiles to connect with family and friends.

feedback Evaluation or information in response to an inquiry.

identity theft The illegal use of someone else's personal information (such as a Social Security number) especially in order to obtain money or credit.

instant messaging A form of real-time, direct, text-based communication between two or more people.

integrity The quality of being honest and having strong moral principles.

internet A network linking computers all over the world; the World Wide Web.

internship A position in which a beginner participates in a program to acquire experience in an occupation, profession, or pursuit.

introvert A quiet person who does not find it easy to talk to other people.

LinkedIn A professional network that allows you to be introduced to and collaborate with other professionals.

mentor An adviser or trusted counselor who can facilitate an individual's personal or professional growth by sharing knowledge and insight.

microblogging Small elements of content sent through websites.

network A collection of computers interconnected in order to share resources and information. Also, the people with whom you share personal and professional information.

objective A purpose or goal set to be achieved by a certain time.

podcast An audio and visual broadcast that is produced for distribution on the internet. Professional organizations (such as news media) and amateur producers share their content on the web.

profession A job that requires special education, training, or skill.

QR code Short for quick response code, a two-dimensional group of shapes that can be read by a scanner.

relationship The way in which two or more people or groups connect together.

search engine A computer program that finds answers to queries from databases on the web.

Twitter A website offering an online social networking and microblogging service of text-based messages of up to 280 characters called tweets.

FOR MORE INFORMATION

American Management Association (AMA)
1601 Broadway
New York, NY 10019
(887) 566-9441
Website: www.amanet.org
This professional organization provides seminars, workshops, and job
opportunity posts for individuals, corporations, and government
agencies.

Conference Board of Canada
255 Smyth Road
Ottawa, ON K1H 8M7
Canada
(866) 711-2262
Website: www.conferenceboard.ca
This independent not-for-profit research organization in Canada promotes
networking skills and develops leadership techniques.

Forté Foundation
9600 Escarpment, Suite 745 PMB 72
Austin, TX 78749
(512) 535-5157
Website: www.fortefoundation.org
The Forté Foundation is a consortium of major corporations and top business schools committed to educating and directing talented women
toward leadership roles in business.

**Future Business Leaders of America-Phi Beta Lambda, Inc.
(FBLA-PBL)**
1912 Association Drive
Reston, VA 20191-1591
(800) 325-2946
Website: www.fbla-pbl.org
FBLA is a nonprofit educational association for students preparing for a
career in business.

LeadAmerica
1515 South Federal Highway, Suite 301
Boca Raton, FL 33432

(866) 394-5323
Website: www.lead-america.org
LeadAmerica arranges conferences for middle school and high school students to explore their interests in an interactive learning environment.

International Association of Women (IAW)
55 E. Monroe Street
Suite 2120
Chicago, IL, 60603
(888) 852-1600
Website: www.iawomen.com
The IAW is a networking forum for women who want to grow their career, promote their business, share ideas, and expand their network.

MENTOR National
201 South Street, Suite 615
Boston, MA 02111
(617) 303-4600
Website: www.mentoring.org
This organization aims to close the mentoring gap and drive equity through quality mentoring relationships for young people.

Small Business Community Network (SBCN)
133 Weber Street N., Suite #3-183
Waterloo, ON N2J 3G9
Canada
(800) 737-5812
Website: www.sbcncanada.org
This Canadian organization provides networking opportunities for small businesses.

Youth Mentoring Connection
4103 W Adams Blvd, 2nd Floor
Los Angeles, CA 90018
(323) 648-8548
Website: www.youthmentoring.org
This organization supports relationships between adults and youth and supports school and work mentoring programs.

FOR FURTHER READING

Bocci, Goali Saedi. *The Social Media Workbook for Teens: Skills to Help You Balance Screen Time, Manage Stress, and Take Charge of Your Life.* Oakland, CA: Instant Help Books, 2019.

Covey, Sean. *The 7 Habits of Highly Effective Teens.* New York, NY: Simon & Schuster, 2014.

Folger, Joseph P., Marshall Scott Poole, and Randall K. Stutman. *Working Through Conflict: Strategies for Relationships, Groups, and Organizations.* New York, NY: Routledge, 2021.

Ford, Jeanne Marie. *Respecting Opposing Viewpoints.* New York, NY: Cavendish Square Publishing, 2018.

Gonzales, Len. *The Truth Behind Social Networking: What Teens, Young Adults, and Parents Need to Know.* Independently published, 2020.

Grillo, Marcela D. *Networking for Teens with Disabilities and Their Allies.* New York, NY: Rosen Young Adult, 2019.

Humphrey, Stephanie T. *Don't Let Your Digital Footprint Kick You in the Butt!* Independently published, 2020.

Kuromiya, Jun. *The Future of Communication.* Minneapolis, MN: Lerner Publications, 2021.

Leonardo, Nixaly. *Active Listening Techniques: 30 Practical Tools to Hone Your Communication Skills.* Emeryville, CA: Rockridge Press, 2020.

McNulty, Laurie Chaikind. *Focus and Thrive: Executive Functioning Strategies for Teens: Tools to Get Organized, Plan Ahead, and Achieve Your Goals.* Emeryville, CA: Rockridge Press, 2020.

Nichols, Michael P., and Martha B. Straus. *The Lost Art of Listening, Third Edition: How Learning to Listen Can Improve Relationships.* New York, NY: The Guilford Press, 2021.

Skeen, Michelle. *Communication Skills for Teens: How to Listen, Express, and Connect for Success.* Oakland, CA: Instant Help Books, 2016.

Van Noord, Maria. *Assertiveness for Teens: 4 Easy to Use Methods to Stop Bullying and to Stand-up for Yourself.* Independently published, 2018.

Wood, Angela, PhD. *The Motivational Interviewing Workbook: Exercises to Decide What You Want and How to Get There.* Emeryville, CA: Rockridge Press, 2020.

INDEX

PHOTO CREDITS

Cover, pp. 17, 66 Monkey Business Images/Shutterstock.com; chapter backgrounds (speech bubbles) en-owai/Shutterstock.com; pp. 5, 9, 49, 64 Rawpixel.com/Shutterstock.com; pp. 12, 63 insta_photos/Shutterstock.com; pp. 13, 26, 30, 38 fizkes/Shutterstock.com; p. 19 GaudiLab/Shutterstock.com; p. 21 Julia Albul/Shutterstock.com; p. 23 Dmytro Zinkevych/Shutterstock.com; pp. 32–33 Sattalat Phukkum/Shutterstock.com; p. 35 (both) Frederic Legrand - COMEO/Shutterstock.com; p. 42 Dragon Images/Shutterstock.com; p. 45 one photo/Shutterstock.com; p. 47 Krakenimages.com/Shutterstock.com; p. 50 Allmy/Shutterstock.com; p. 53 Maksim Shmeljov/Shutterstock.com; p. 56 OPOLJA/Shutterstock.com; p. 58 Bojan Milinkov/Shutterstock.com; p. 61 sirtravelalot/Shutterstock.com; p. 69 UfaBizPhoto/Shutterstock.com.

Editor: Greg Roza
Designer: Michael Flynn